Walking in the Forest

By Rose Lily

Illustrated by Judy DuFour Love

Target Skill Setting

PEARSON

Scott
Foresman

Tam is walking with
Mom and Dad.

Tam sees a beaver.

Tam spots a frog.

Tam sees a nest
with one duck.

Tam sees a fox on the rock.

Tam spots a big bird.

They have lots of pictures!